Sharon, Lois & Bram
Sing A to Z

SHARON, LOIS & BRAM
SING A TO Z

❖

Pictures by Kim LaFave

Crown Publishers, Inc.

New York

Musical arrangements by Eddie Graf
Text and musical arrangements copyright © 1991 by
Elephant Records Inc. Illustrations copyright © 1991 by
Kim LaFave

Manufactured in Hong Kong

Library of Congress Cataloging-in-Publication Data
Sharon, Lois, and Bram.
Sharon, Lois & Bram sing A to Z / illustrated by Kim LaFave.
1 score.
Children's songs from the record album; with piano acc.
Includes index.
1. Children's songs.   I. LaFave, Kim, ill. II. Title.
III. Title: Sharon, Lois, and Bram sing A to Z.
IV. Title: Sing A to Z.
M1992.S515S5   1992   91-18990
ISBN 0-517-58723-8 (paperback)
10 9 8 7 6 5 4 3 2 1
First U.S. Edition

Cover photography by Gordon Hay
Design by Michael Solomon
Printed and bound in Hong Kong

MUSIC CREDITS

"Baby Face" by Harry Akst, Benny Davis. © 1926 by
Warner Bros. Inc. (Renewed). Used by permission.
All rights reserved.

"Come Follow the Band" by Cy Coleman, Michael
Stewart. © 1959 Notable Music Company Inc. All
rights administered by WB Music Corp. Used by
permission. All rights reserved.

"Cubanola Glide" by Harry Von Tilzer. Used by
permission of Polygram Music Publishing Co.

"Lollipop" (original title "Harrigan") by George M.
Cohan. Used by permission of George M. Cohan
Music Pub. Co.

"Jellyman Kelly" by James Taylor. © 1980 by Country
Road Music Inc. Used by permission. All rights
reserved.

"Little Sir Echo" by John S. Fearis, Laura Rountree
Smith. Revised version by Adele Girard and Joe
Marsala. © 1944 WB Music Corp. (Renewed). Used
by permission. All rights reserved.

"Mairzy Doats" by Milton Drake, Al Hoffman, Jerry
Livingstone. © 1943 Miller Music Corp. © 1971
renewed and assigned to Hallmark Music Co. Inc.,
Beverly Hills, CA. International copyright secured. All
rights reserved.

"The Name Game" by Shirley Elliston, Lincoln
Chase. © 1964 Al Gallico Music Corp., New York,
NY. International copyright secured. All rights
reserved.

"New World Coming." Words and music by Barry
Mann and Cynthia Weil. © 1970 Screen Gems-EMI
Music Inc. Used by permission. All rights reserved.

"Owl Lullaby" by Stan Jones. © 1951, 1952 Edwin
H. Morris & Company. © renewed 1979, 1980
Edwin H. Morris & Company, a division of MPL
Communications Inc. International copyright secured.
All rights reserved.

"Somebody Come and Play" by Joe Raposo. © 1970
Jonico Music Inc. International copyright secured. All
rights reserved.

"Tzena Tzena" by Julius Grossman, Issachor Miron
and Mitchell Parish. © 1950 by Mills Music Inc.
© renewed c/o Filmtrax Copyright Holdings Inc. Used
by permission. All rights reserved.

SHARON, LOIS & BRAM
SING A TO Z

TABLE OF CONTENTS

THE ALPHABET SONG

(sung to the tune of "Twinkle, Twinkle, Little Star")

Now I know my ABC's,
Next time won't you sing with me.

ABC JIG

Light and Bright

Mary had a little lamb, its fleece was white as snow,
And everywhere that Mary went the lamb was sure to go.

Oh, ABCDEFGHIJKLM
NOPQRSTUVWXYZ

8

Little Miss Muffet
sat on a tuffet,
eating her curds and whey;
Along came a spider
and sat down beside her
and frightened Miss Muffet away.

Oh, ABCDEFGHIJKLM
NOPQRSTUVWXYZ

Jack be nimble, Jack be quick,
Jack jump over the candlestick.

Oh, ABCDEFGHIJKLM
NOPQRSTUVWXYZ

The grand old Duke of York, he had ten
    thousand men;
He marched them up to the top of the hill
    and he marched them down again.
And when they were up they were up, and
    when they were down they were down,
And when they were only half way up they
    were neither up nor down.

Oh, ABCDEFGHIJKLM
NOPQRSTUVWXYZ

9

is for big, brass band.

Come follow me, come follow me;
Put one foot in front of the other foot and follow me.

COME FOLLOW THE BAND

Moderate 2

D11　　　　　　G　　　　　　　　　　Am7　　D7

Come fol-low the band, _____ Wher - ev - er it's at; _____ Let both of your feet

G　　B7　　C/E　　C　　　A7　　　　D7

_____ beat　　time to the drum　And feel your heart go rat - a - tat - tat;　A　flag in your hand,

G　　　　　　Am7　　D7　　　　　G　　B7

_____ A　plume in your hat, _____ Bat - tal-ions of brass _____ pass　and

C6　　C#dim　　G/D　　D7　　　G　　　F#7

catch　the light -　Is there a　sight that's swee-ter than that?　See the pret - ty la - dy

B7　　　　　　　　　　　　　　　Em

toss　that　ba - ton　high; _____ Ain't　she　cute　as　a　dai - sy? _____

10

Watch the fel - la with the   big bass drum go by;___ Ain't you glad that you   stayed?

Hear the tu - ba play that   oom-pah - pah; Oh my, ___ Ain't it driv - in' you   cra - zy?

Don't you be so darn   la - zy. _____ You bet - ter hur-ry and   join that big par - ade.

___ Up out of your seat, _____ Down off of the stand, _____ Out in - to the crowd

_____ loud with   hip hoo - ray, ___ A sound that   you'll   re - mem - ber

all your days,   And when you see   that lea - der   proud - ly   raise   his

ha - a - a - a - and,   Come   fol - low the

band. _____

11

CHICK, CHICK, CHICKEN

Chick, chick, chick, chick, chicken,
Lay a little egg for me.

Chick, chick, chick, chick, chicken,
I want one for my tea.

I haven't had an egg since Easter,
And now it's half past three.

Oh, chick, chick, chick, chicken,
Lay a little egg for me.

C - H - I - C - K - E - N

Moderato

C - is the way to be-gin, and H - is the next let-ter in, and

I - is the mid-dle of the word, and C - you've al-read-y heard, and

K - is a kind of a hen, and E - get-ting near the end ___

C - H - I - C - K - E - N ___ - that's the way you spell chick-en.

12

HAM AND EGGS

Ham and eggs, ham and eggs, I like mine fried nice and brown; And I like mine turned up-side-down. Ham and eggs, ham and eggs, Flip flop, flip flop, Ham and eggs.

13

makes me want to dance, dee-dee dee-dee DEE DEE.

THE CUBANOLA GLIDE

Allegro moderato

Way down in Cu - ba where skies are clear, And it is sum - mer - time

all of the year. They got the lov - in' - est dance I know;

Come a - long, hon - ey babe, and I'll show you: Get a - way clo - ser, hon,

squeeze me tight, Rag - a - tag to ___ the left, then to the right,

Shake it up, shake it up, side by side, Cud-dle right up ___ to me

15

as we slide. Ain't it en - tran - cin', when you're a - dan - cin'

Chorus

That Cu - ba - no - la Glide. Glide, glide keep on a - glid - in',

Slide, slide keep on a - slid - in', Ho - ney, look in - to your

ba - by's eyes, _____ throw your arms a - round me, Ain't you glad you found me,

Tease, squeeze, lov - in' and woo - in', Oh, babe,

what are you do - in'? Ride to glo - ry by your ba - by's side _____

When you do __ the Cu - ba - no - la Glide.

I'm going crazy, hon, hear that band;
Ain't it a daisy, it's certainly grand;
Never heard music like that before.
Rag it some more and we'll glide to glory,
Pucker your rosy lips, lift the lid,

Throw me a lovin' kiss, oh you kid;
Honey bunch, honey bunch, whisper low,
Tell me that you love me, babe, let me know.
I feel so spoony, I'm going loony,
Don't ever let me go.

17

LITTLE SIR ECHO

Little Sir Echo, you're very near;
Hello (hello), hello (hello).
Little Sir Echo, you're very dear;
Hello (hello), hello (hello).

frog

GATGOON

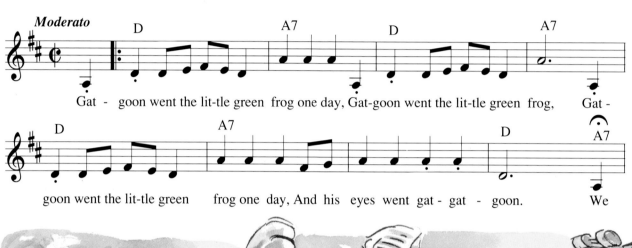

Moderato

Gat - goon went the lit-tle green frog one day, Gat-goon went the lit-tle green frog, Gat -

goon went the lit-tle green frog one day, And his eyes went gat - gat - goon. We

all know frogs go la - de-da - de-da, La - de-da - de-da, la - de-da - de-da, We

all know frogs go la - de-da - de-da, They don't go gat - gat - goon. Gat - goon!

FIVE LITTLE FISHIES

Five little fishies
Swimming in the pool,
The first one said,
This pool is cool.
The second one said,
This pool is deep.
The third one said,
I think I'll sleep.
The fourth one said,
Let's swim and dip.
The fifth one said,
I see a ship.
The fisherman's line
　　went
Splish, splish, splash,
And away the five
Little fishies dash!

22

LES PETITS POISSONS

Les pet - tits pois - sons dans l'eau, Na - gent, na - gent, na - gent, na - gent;

_____ Les pet - tits pois - sons dans l'eau, Na - gent, nag' de bas en haut. _____

All the fishes in the sea,
They are swimming, swimming, swimming;
Oh, the fishes swimming round,
Swimming up and swimming down.

Les petits oiseaux du soir,
Volent, volent, volent, volent;
Les petits oiseaux du soir,
Volent, volent dans les airs.

All the birdies in the night,
They go flying, flying, flying;
All the birdies in the sky,
Flying low and flying high.

Le rouet de grand-maman
   Oh, Grandma's spinning wheel,
File, file, file, file;
   Turning, turning, turning, turning.
   Grandma's spinning wheel,
   Turning round and round and round.
Le rouet de grand-maman
File, file doucement.

23

GRANDPA'S FARM

Down on Grandpa's farm there is a fat pink pig,
Down on Grandpa's farm there is a fat pink pig;
The pig, it goes a lot like this: *oink, oink*;
The pig, it goes a lot like this: *oink, oink*.   *Chorus*

Down on Grandpa's farm there is a milk white cow,
Down on Grandpa's farm there is a milk white cow;
The cow, it goes a lot like this: *moo, moo*;
The cow, it goes a lot like this: *moo, moo*.

    Chorus

Down on Grandpa's farm there is an old red rooster,
Down on Grandpa's farm there is an old red rooster;
The rooster, it goes a lot like this: *cock-a-doodle-doo*;
The rooster, it goes a lot like this: *cock-a-doodle-doo*.

Down on Grandpa's farm there is an old time band,
Down on Grandpa's farm there is an old time band;
The band, it goes a lot like this: (*band playing*);
The band, it goes a lot like this: (*band playing*).

    Chorus

    Chorus

25

horse, of course!

Shoe a little horse,
Shoe a little mare,
But let the little coltie
Go bare, bare, bare.

CABALLITO BLANCO

Cab - al - li - to blan - co, lle - va me de a - quí;

Lle - va me a mi pue - blo Don - de yo na - ci.

Ten - go, ten - go, ten - go, Tu no tien - es na - da;

Ten - go tres o - ve - jas En u - na ca - ba - ña.

Una me da leche,
Otra me da lana,
Otra mantequilla
Para la semana.

Little white horse,
Carry me away;
Take me back to the village
Where I was born.
I have many things,
You have nothing;
I have three sheep in the barn.
One gives me milk,
Another gives me wool,
The other, butter for the whole
    week.

I scream, you scream,   we all scream for iceworms.

WHEN THE ICEWORMS NEST AGAIN

Verse 1

There's a trusty husky maiden in the Arctic, And she waits for me, but it is not in vain; For some night I'll put my mukluks on and ask her If she'll wed me when the iceworms nest again.

Chorus

In the land of the pale blue snow, Where it's ninety-nine below, And the polar bears go rolling o'er the plain; In the shadow of the pole, I'll clasp her to my soul: We'll be married when the iceworms nest again.

For our wedding feast we'll have seal oil and blubber,
In our kayak we will sail the bounding main;
All the walruses will look at us and rubber,
We'll be married when the iceworms nest again.

Chorus

My name is Jenny,
And my husband's name is Johnny,

And we come from
New Jersey
With a carload of jelly.

JELLYMAN KELLY

Moderato

C ... A7

1. Here's a sto - ry 'bout Jel - ly-man Kel-ly, He loves jel- ly the most; _____ But

D9 ... G7 ... C ... G7

most of all _____ Jel - ly - man Kel - ly loves jel - ly on toast.

C ... A7

Here's the part a - bout Jen-ny Mul-hen-ny, She's a fi - re - man's daugh-ter; ___ But

D9 ... G7 ... C ... G7

most of all _____ Jen - ny Mul - hen - ny likes to boil hot wa - ter. **2.** So,

30

3. Jen-ny, put the ket-tle on.   Jel- ly-man Kel-ly, won't you come home? Jel-ly, won't you come.

Oh,   can he   come home, Jen-ny? Can he come home, Jen-ny, can he   come?

Oh,   can he   come home, Jen-ny? Can he come home, Jen- ny, can he   come?

Fine

Here's a sto - ry 'bout   Jel - ly-man Kel-ly,   He loves jel- ly the   most; _____ And

D.S. al Fine

may-be some-day _____ You and me, we could have   tea with him. ___

31

I get a kick out of K.

KIDDY KUM KIMO

Moderato

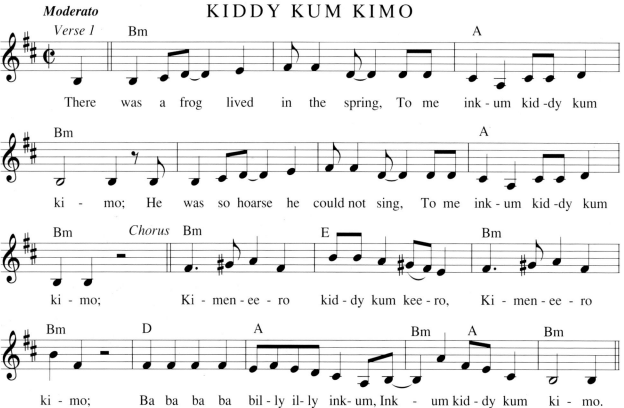

Verse 1 | Bm | A

There was a frog lived in the spring, To me ink - um kid -dy kum

Bm | A

ki - mo; He was so hoarse he could not sing, To me ink - um kid -dy kum

Bm | *Chorus* Bm | E | Bm

ki - mo; Ki - men - ee - ro kid -dy kum kee - ro, Ki - men - ee - ro

Bm | D | A | Bm | A | Bm

ki - mo; Ba ba ba ba bil - ly il- ly ink- um, Ink - um kid -dy kum ki - mo.

Well I called that frog and he jumped out,
To me inkum kiddy kum kimo;
He hopped and he skipped and he danced
   all about,
To me inkum kiddy kum kimo.

Chorus

Way down yonder in possum creek,
To me inkum kiddy kum kimo,
The fellas grow to be ten feet,
To me inkum kiddy kum kimo.

Chorus

They tried to sleep but it's no use,
To me inkum kiddy kum kimo,
'Cause their feet stick out for the hens
   to roost,
To me inkum kiddy kum kimo.

Chorus

Well, the songbook's lying on the shelf,
To me inkum kiddy kum kimo;
If you want any more you can sing it yourself,
To me inkum kiddy kum kimo.

Chorus

33

L is for love.

BABY FACE

Rosy cheeks and turned up nose and curly hair,
I'm raving 'bout my baby now,
Pretty little dimples here and dimples there,
Don't want to live without her,
I love her, goodness knows;
They wrote this song about her
And here's the way it goes:

Chorus
Baby face,
You've got the cutest little baby face,
There's not another one to take your place,
Baby face;
My poor heart is jumpin',
You sure have started somethin';
Baby face,
I'm up in heaven when I'm in your fond embrace;
I didn't need a shove
'Cause I just fell in love
With your pretty baby face.

When you were a baby not so long ago,
You must have been the cutest thing;
I can picture you at every baby show,
Just winnin' every ribbon
With your sweet baby ways;
Say, honest, I ain't fibbin',
You'd win them all today.

Chorus

34

MAIRZY DOATS

I know a ditty, nutty as a fruitcake,
Goofy as a goon and silly as a loon.
Some call it pretty, others call it crazy,
But they all sing this tune:

Mair - zy doats and do-zy doats and lid - dle lam-zy di-vey, A kid-dl-ey di-vey too, would-n't

you? Mair - zy doats and do - zy doats and lid - dle lam-zy di - vey, A

kid- dl -ey div-ey too, would - n't you? Well, if the words sound queer, and

fun - ny to your ear, A lit - tle bit jumb-led and ji-vey, Sing "mares eat oats and

does eat oats, and lit - tle lambs eat i - vy." Oh!

36

Mair - zy doats and do - zy doats and lid - dle lam-zy di - vey, A kid-dl-ey div-ey too, would-n't

you - oo - oo - hoo! A kid - dl - ey div - ey too, would - n't you?

Whailzy deals and sealzy deals and baby fishy doysters,
A squiddley doysters too, wouldn't you?

If the words sound queer, and funny to your ear,
All of you girlsters and boysters
Say "whales eat eels and seals eat eels
And baby fish eat oysters."

Whales eat eels and seals eat eels and baby fish eat oysters,
A squid will eat oysters too, wouldn't you?

A whale will eat oysters too,
A squid will eat oysters too,
A kid will eat ivy too, wouldn't you?

37

"N" my name is Natasha
And my husband's name is Nathan,
And we come from Nairobi
With a carload of names.

THE NAME GAME

Bright Rock 4

Come on, ev'-ry-bo-dy, I say now, let's play a game. I bet you

I can make a rhyme Out of an-y-bo-dy's name. Like

Shir-ley, Shir-ley, bo Bir-ley, Bo-na-na fa-na fo Fir-ley, me migh mo Mir-ley, Shir-ley.

The first letter of the name
Is treated like it wasn't there,
But a B or an F or an M will appear;
Then I say bo, add a be and then I say the name,
And then bonana fana with a fo.
And then I say the name again with an F very plain,
Then a me migh and mo.
Then I say the name again with an M this time,
And there isn't any name that I can't rhyme.

Sharon, Sharon bo Baron,
Bonana fana fo Faron,
Me migh mo Maron,
Sharon!

Lois, Lois bo Bois,
Bonana fana fo Fois,
Me migh mo Mois,
Lois!

Bram, Bram bo Bram,
Bonana fana fo Fam,
Me migh mo Mam,
Bram!

38

But if the first two letters are ever the same,
Then you drop them both and say the name.

Bob, Bob drop the B bo ob;
Fred, Fred drop the F fo red;
Mary, Mary drop the M mo ary;
That's the only rule that is contrary.

Ok? Now say bo (BO),
Now Tony with a B (BONY),
Bonana fana fo (BONANA FANA FO);
Then you say the name again with an F very plain (FONY),
Then a me migh and mo (ME MIGH MO)
Then you say the name again with an M this time (MONY),
And there isn't any name that you can't rhyme.

is an owl.

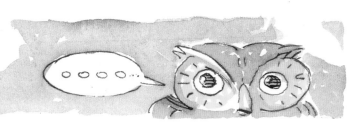

OWL LULLABY

Intro

Chorus

Who, who, who? _____ Who will talk to me? Who will

ans - wer me? Who knows why I sing who? Who, _____ who knows the

Verse

rea - son why I sing this lul - la - by? Who, who, who? _____ The

owls ____ are fly - ing, I hear them all sigh - ing Through the trees and the

cur - tains as they hur - ry on home; _____ With my feet on a limb and my

eyes sad and lone - ly I sing who, who, who? _____

Who will talk to me? Who will ans - wer me? Who knows

why I sing who? Who, who, who, who knows the rea - son why

I sing this lul - la - by? Who, who, who? _____

SUSANNAH'S A FUNNY OLD MAN

Bright Waltz

C   Dm7   G7

There was an old man and he had an old sow, *(snort)* - ow *(pft)*

G7   C   Dm

- ow *(wht)* - aye did - dle dow; There was an old man and he had an old

G7   *Slower*   D7   G7   *a tempo* C

sow, Las - si - fer - rall - de - ran; Oh, Su - san - nah's a

G7   C   C

fun - ny old man. *(snort)* - an *(pft)* - an *(wht)* - an Su - san - nah's a

G7   C   C ·   F

fun - ny old man. _____ Sing cheer - ful, bright and

C   G7   C   A7

gay, _____ Sing hap - pi - ly all of the day. _____ Su -

Dm7   G7   C

san - nah's a fun - ny old man. *(snort)* - an *(pft)* - an *(wht)*

C   G7   C

- an Su - san - nah's a fun - ny old man. _____

Now this old sow had nine little pigs, *(snort)*-iggs, *(pft)*-iggs,
(wht)-aye-diddle-digs;
Now this old sow she had nine little pigs,
Lacifer-rall-da-ran;   *Chorus*

They tried to climb over the garden wall, *(snort)*-all, *(pft)*-all,
(wht)-aye-diddle-doll;
They tried to climb over the garden wall,   *pft = raspberry*
Lacifer-rall-da-ran;   *Chorus*   *wht = whistle*

43

P is for play.

Happy hearts and happy faces;
Happy play in grassy places.

WHAT SHALL WE DO WHEN WE ALL GO OUT?

What shall we do when we all go out,
All go out, all go out,
What shall we do when we all go out,
When we all go out to play?

We will ride on our three-wheeled bikes,
Three-wheeled bikes, three-wheeled bikes,
We will ride on our three-wheeled bikes
When we all go out to play.

SOMEBODY COME
AND PLAY

Somebody come and play,
Somebody come and play today;
Somebody come and smile the smiles
And sing the songs, it won't take long,
Somebody come and play today.

Somebody come and play,
Somebody come and play my way;
Somebody come and rhyme the rhymes
And laugh the laughs, it won't take time,
Somebody come and play today.

Somebody come with me,
We'll see the pleasure in the wind;
Somebody come before it gets
Too late to begin.

Somebody come and play,
Somebody come and play my way;
Somebody come and be my friend
And watch the sun 'til it rains again,
Somebody come and play today.

45

HUSH, LITTLE BABY

Gently

Hush, lit-tle ba-by, don't say a word, Mom-ma's gon-na buy you a mock-ing - bird;

If that mock-ing - bird won't sing, Mom-ma's gon-na buy you a dia-mond ring;

If that dia - mond ring turns brass, Mom-ma's gon-na buy you a look-ing glass;

If that look-ing glass gets broke, Mom-ma's gon-na buy you a bil - ly goat; So

(last time)

Coda: slower

hush, lit-tle ba-by, don't you cry, Dad - dy loves you and so do I.

If that billy goat won't pull,
Momma's gonna buy you a cart and bull;
If that cart and bull turn over,
Momma's gonna buy you a dog named Rover;
If that dog named Rover won't bark,
Momma's gonna buy you a horse and cart;
If that horse and cart fall down,
You'll still be the sweetest little baby in town.
So hush, little baby, don't you cry,
Daddy loves you and so do I.

46

"rr" con "rr"
"rr" with "rr" — cigar
"rr" with "rr" — barrel
Rapidly run the cars
Of the railway train.

RIDING IN THE BUGGY/TIDEO

(in 2)

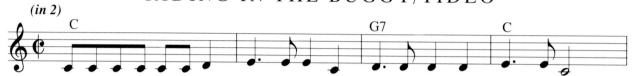

Rid-ing in the bug-gy, Miss Ma - ry Jane, Miss Ma - ry Jane, Miss Ma - ry Jane,

Rid-ing in the bug-gy, Miss Ma - ry Jane, long way from home.

Come ride with me, Come ride with me,

C ... **G7** ... **C**

Come ride with me, my dar - ling, Come ride with me.

TIDEO

C ... sim.

Skip one win - dow, Ti - de - o, Skip two win - dows, Ti - de - o,

Skip three win - dows, Ti - de - o, Jin - gle at the win - dows, Ti - de - o,

G7 / C

Ti - de - o, Ti - de - o, Jin - gle at the win - dows, Ti - de - o,

Fair thee well, my little bitty Ann,
My little bitty Ann, my little bitty Ann;
Fair thee well, my little bitty Ann,
I must be on my way.

Chorus

Don't know when I'm coming back,
Coming back, coming back;
Don't know when I'm coming back,
But I'll be back some day.

S is for spelling. Banananana

I know how to spell.   BANANA – ba na na na na na.   I just don't know when to stop.

SPELLING MEDLEY

Moderate 2   *Lollipop*

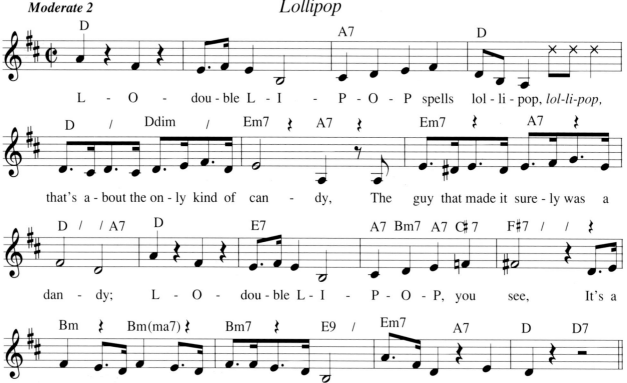

L - O - dou-ble L-I - P - O - P spells lol-li-pop, *lol-li-pop,*

that's a-bout the on-ly kind of can - dy,   The   guy that made it sure-ly was   a

dan - dy;   L - O - dou-ble L-I - P - O - P, you   see,   It's a

lick   on   a stick Guar-an-teed to make you sick,   Lol-li-pop   that's   me.

50

Chorus
That was a cute little rhyme;
Spell us another one,
Just like the other one,
Spell us another one, do.

S-M-I-L-E

It is - n't a - ny trou - ble just to S - M - I - L - E, It

is - n't a - ny trou - ble just to S - M - I - L - E, So

smile a - way your trou - ble, It will van - ish like a bub - ble If you

on - ly take the trou - ble just to S - M - I - L - E.

51

W-A-L-K, Walk

Let's take a W - A - L - K walk in the P - A - R - K

park And I will K - I - S - S kiss you in the D - A - R - K dark, And I will

L - O - V - E love you all the T - I - M - E time, And I will

nev - er, nev - er leave you for a D - I - M - E dime.

Chorus
That was a cute little rhyme;
We'll spell another one,
Just like the other one,
If you will spell along too.

Bingo

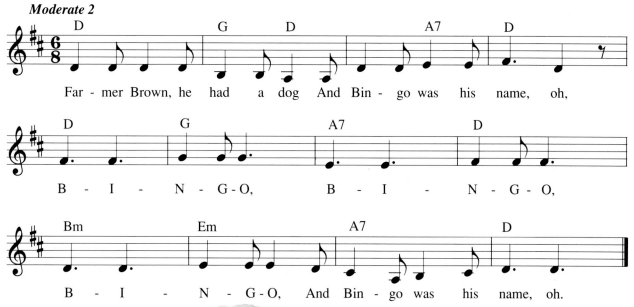

Moderate 2

| D | G | D | A7 | D |

Far - mer Brown, he had a dog And Bin - go was his name, oh,

| D | G | A7 | D |

B - I - N - G-O, B - I - N - G-O,

| Bm | Em | A7 | D |

B - I - N - G-O, And Bin - go was his name, oh.

MISTER SUN

Oh, Mister Sun, Sun,
Mister Golden Sun,
Won't you please shine down on me?
Oh, Mister Sun, Sun,
Mister Golden Sun,
Hiding behind a tree.

Boys and girls, I'm telling you
To campsong singing you better be true.
Oh, Mister Sun, Sun,
Mister Golden Sun,
Won't you please shine down on me?

TZENA, TZENA

Bright 2

1. Tze - na, tze - na, tze - na, tze - na, Can't you hear the mu - sic play-ing In _____

_____ the ci - ty square _____ Tze - na, tze - na, tze - na, tze - na,

Come where all our friends will find us With _____ the dan-cers there. _____

2. Tze - na, tze - na, join the cel - e - bra - tion, There'll be peo - ple there from

ev' - ry na - tion. Dawn will find us laugh - ing in the

sun - light, Dan - cing in the ci - ty square. _____

3. Tze - na, tze - na, come and dance the ho - ra, One, two, three, four;

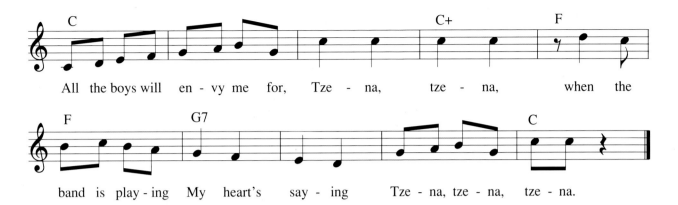

All the boys will en - vy me for, Tze - na, tze - na, when the

band is play - ing My heart's say - ing Tze - na, tze - na, tze - na.

Tzena, tzena, tzena, tzena,
Habanot urena chayalim bamoshava.
Alna, Alna, Alna, Alna,
Alna titchabena mi ben chayil ish tzava.

Tzena, tzena
Habanot urena chayalim bamoshava.
Alna, Alna,
Alna titchabena mi ben chayil ish tzava.

Tzena, tzena, tzena, tzena, tzena, tzena, tzena,
Tzena, tzena, tzena, tzena, tzena, tzena, tzena,
Tzena, tzena, tzena, tzena, tzena, tzena, tzena,

Tzena, tzena, come and dance the hora,
One, two, three, four.
All the boys will envy me for,
Tzena, tzena, when the band is playing
My heart's saying tzena, tzena, tzena.

UP IN THE AIR, JUNIOR BIRDSMEN

Up in the air, we're jun-ior birds-men, Up in the air, up-side down; Up in the air, _____ we're jun-ior birds-men, We keep our nos-es to the ground. And when you hear _____ the grand an-nounce-ment That our wings are made of tin, Then you will know the jun-ior birds-men Have sent their box-tops in. It takes five box-tops, Four bot-tle bot-toms, Three la-bels, Two cou-pons, And one thin di-i-me.

56

57

58